Keep It Elite

The Game Changing Mentality

JAHVON GORDON

The author is represented by Worth It Publishing, LLC
Worth It Publishing, LLC
1770 E Street, NE
Washington DC, 20002

Printed in the United States of America
First Edition: August 2014

ISBN-13: 978-1499188080

ISBN-10:1499188080

Editor- Dr. Janice Armstrong
Photo credit: Jackie Armstrong Photography:
www.jackiearmstrong.com
Cover Design: One Accord Events' Graphic Team:
www.OneAccordEvents.com

http://www.merriam-webster.com/dictionary/satisfaction

CONTENTS

Dedication and Thank You
Foreword by Dr. Mike Freeman
Introduction by Dr. Eric Cooper

DEDICATION

Thank God that I am one of the saved; my life is a true living testimony to what one of my favorite scriptures say: "Called out of darkness into His marvelous light"- 1 Peter 2:9. It's amazing when I think about how I got to this place and how I am able to maintain. This testimony shows me that it is clearly God that has done it. First, I would like to thank my Mom and Dad. Both of you have deposited so many different things into me, all in which I have taken into careful consideration and formatted a life that is conducive to living in excellence. Separately, you two have done what was thought to be impossible. Mom, you gave your soul to see this day and guess what? It is here. Dad, you sacrificed the latter parts of life's promises and have seen to it that the work my mother put into place would not go to waste. I believe that internally, you both have done a wonderful job on this one. I believe that it began the day you decided within yourselves that Jahvon Juan Gordon would see the light of day. Regardless of time physically spent, for you both have missed moments equally, I love you both for what you have done. This book is what has resulted in your willingness to open your heart to tell me, "Yes!" To my Grandma and Grandpa, you are the two most important people in my memory bank. Although Grandpa Ed is gone, I still ruminate on his loving rub on the crown of my head right after I used to burst through his newspaper. Grandma, I have vowed to be just as giving as you for the rest of my life. There is no one person that loves me more than you. I will forever be thankful to you two. This book is dedicated to my beautiful, bodacious wife, Temica "My Cornbread Shawty". I appreciate how you have shared this space with me as we have fought the good fight, and now stand strong as a unit exemplifying love and resilience in such a dark time in the history of marriages. I appreciate your growth and maturity, your kindness and patience, your candor as you have developed into such a terrific wife and friend. I love you for you, and you alone. I want Maddy, Jahnia and Jahvonnie to know that their daddy has made the impossible, possible, through the following of the voice of the Holy Spirit. He has guided my every thought and submission of this book and shown me the probabilities that exist for those that are faithful. Kids, you are part of an Empire that is never to be broken, never to be forgotten, and never to be rendered as useless. Utilize this example as a way to create a future that matters not only to you but for those that will build upon the Gordon legacy.

I inherited a family in Nikki, Theresa, Mary,

Andrea, Omar, Debra and the rest of the crew. You all have pushed, fought, cried and laughed with me as I have grown alongside you. No one man could have received a better set of tribesmen. Your holistic approach to sharing and supporting is like 7/11; it never stops growing. I really appreciate having you all in my life. And to my brothers Robert and Derrick, you guys are more than just brothers, but my twins. There is an inseparable bond between us and it shows its awesomeness in every conversation that we have. You have, in your own ways, impressed me with your followership and your tenacity in your own endeavors. I couldn't have asked for a better pair of brothers than you; therefore, I say "thank you" for continuing to breathe and dream with me. Rob, thanks for the Redskins/Cowboys jersey you wear with my name on your back. You continue to be a dad and brother to me and for me, even at my age. I will never forget My long drunken nights you shared with me

from miles away when I cried in my misunderstanding of life. Your sweet and caring heartfelt words still resonate within my soul. And to Derrick, know that you have never failed me as a little brother but rather, you have exceeded my expectations by testing the waters. Every single thing that I have exposed to you, you have taken it and have run with it. This has revealed the submissive side of you and how you are ready to grow in every moment. This book is not only a testament of trials that I have faced, but also one filled with the stepping blocks of your past and future. You have lived every moment with me and I look forward to what is next for you young man. #KeepItElite To all of my fraternal brothers from the Mighty Country B.O.E, each of you has influenced me in a mighty way. If anyone could tell my story, it would be the gentlemen from

University of Maryland Eastern Shore and Bowie State. Your heart's dearest thought is what has kept me and your relentlessness to stand by the shield is what has sustained our friendships. Let us continue to strive towards perfecting Christian Manhood, keeping what is essential close, and allowing the one True God to be the one we live to serve first as Omega Men. And lastly but certainly not least, Dr. Freeman; "more is caught than is taught", sir. I have taken the time to submit myself to you, and you alone, and it has paid off. Because I have chosen to listen to your words and follow your path, I have received the Godly counsel from so many Mighty Men Of Valor. Beginning with Dr. Eric Cooper, who taught me to "See Right, Sow Right, and Serve Right" by way of Pastor Dewayne Freeeman. Dr. Cooper pushed this book out of me while showing me the importance of serving even when you don't know why. Mr. Richard Smith, Esq, who has given and given and given into my marriage foundation, which, in turn, has supplied a foundation that keeps on giving. Mr. Henry Armstrong, Ronnie Griffin, Curtis Binion, and Sean Joyner, who have been big brothers that won't give up on me.

Dr. Freeman your vision is what has allowed for my dreams to exist in the earth. Your continued faithfulness in excellence is what has given way for my family to have a church home since the early 90's. There is no one book that I could truly write that could express the gratitude that I have for you and your darling wife, Dr. Dee Dee. I love you both!

Keep It Elite

FORWARD

It gives me great joy to present to you a book that is life changing and challenging. In "Keep it Elite" you will experience the life journey of a young man who exercised his faith and walked out the principles that have led him to the good life that God pre-ordained for all of us. While unfortunately many young men have the propensity to draw back after a setback this book will help guide you and encourage you to keep moving ahead. Jahvon has not only learned these life changing principles but is assisting me in ministry leading other young men to their set place and destiny.

- Dr. Michael A. Freeman

Keep It Elite

Introduction

There comes a time in every male child's life when he makes the transition into a man. For some this metamorphosis happens later in life. Some are forced prematurely into manhood because of family needs. Then there is a group of young men that become the "man of the house" because of the absence of a father, a father figure or male influence in the home. The peril is when it does not happen at all. They are then merely a boy trapped in a man's body. Still talking like a child, behaving like a child, and thinking like a child. Paul said "when I became a man I put away childish things." They unfortunately never do. In 'Keep it Elite' author Jahvon Gordon shares his heart, his journey into manhood and principles that are life changing. This book is a must read for every man and the women that love them.

Dr. Eric Cooper
Author
 Perils of a Silent Man
&
Daddy I Miss You

ELITE

Elite is defined as "being the best of the best; the choice part of a thing". Being "Elite" is not about money, title, station, nor status it is about a choice. #KeepItElite

Keep It Elite

There is no mathematical sequence that has been discovered or uncovered to help and assist people in making their minds up when deciding to live better, have more, and envision more. You can persuade and suggest, but ultimately, it is solely up to that person to make the decision. We see it all the time in the news or we hear it on the street: " 'So and So' is the newest, hottest thing...", then 2 years later, they have fallen off due to some strange thing that shouldn't have happened to them.

My thought is that the #1 cause of every fall from greatness is sin. No one man can avoid it but all men can escape it. The solution to every problem with sin is, simply, a made-up mind. A person's mind must be made up to do the right thing, meanwhile, maintaining the same posture, regardless of what happens and what comes up. This is what I call "Keeping It Elite". With every

4

success story there is always the potential for an unfavorable end. This happens because most people never start out with the end in mind. One should start out with the mindset that, regardless of what comes my way I will always "Keep it Elite".

This book will walk you through some very practical scenarios and object lessons that I have discovered to work so that when you make it to your next wealthy place; you won't fall but

YOU WILL KEEP IT ELITE!

CHAPTER ONE

MISERY BRINGS PLENTY

In 2008 I began a journey like no other. This journey led me into a place that, now, I can say was the best path for me. It was hard, yet fair. Understand that "hard" really means "so bad that I wanted to just die and go to heaven so that all of my misery would be over and done with". It was not hard because other people made it hard or life was just too much for me to handle but rather because I refused to develop into being Elite. This journey is now what I have discovered to be a process. This process has caused me to understand and value developmental phases. At this point I had drawn so far away from the good and gracious place that I once was at that I really didn't know who I was anymore. There was a time in my life when everything I did, I did it with the right intent mainly because I had the correct mindset. My mind was set on doing good and the results of this good brought me plenty of great things. It wasn't until I was no longer satisfied with the results that many of my ways changed. It wasn't the environment I was in or the people that I was around; it simply was my heart and my mind being set on evil. I allowed circumstances and situations to dictate how I saw the world. My life began to shift because I allowed it and in a strange way I liked where it was going. I liked the mean side of me, the evil nature that got revenge whenever possible. I felt like for once in my life I was fighting back against the life that I was born into. I was rebelling and my rebellion resulted in infinite amounts of sin that entered into my heart and mind. It was not until September of 2008 that my rebellion could no longer sustain me and my world came crashing down. It's crazy to think but a large amount of people use their evil ways to win in life; the bad thing is that most evildoers make a very

good run. My mom would often say "keep

doing wrong, lying, stealing and killing and you'll see – it'll catch up to you". I never really knew how deep this could go until all of my mess caught up to me. I can remember lying on the hard wood floor in this apartment, surrounded by musical instruments and boxes. At this time I was working, making $9 an hour as a receptionist while watching a once pretty, prominent promoters career go swishing down the drain. Prior to this, I was living with a bunch of friends but our contract ended and we had to go. You would think that the logical thing for me to do would have been to get with one of the guys and move together but "nope, no bueno". When you lead a life that is corrupt, and is full of cheating all the while you're screwing people over, no one will be interested in trusting you nor will they stand with you. No matter how fun I thought I was as a party promoter/ "master playa", the truth was that no one truly wanted to deal with a guy like me. During this time in November of 2008, while being penalized on this hard wood floor, I was a young man that had become a monster not only to all women, my daughter Madison, her mother, my family, my friends, but also to myself. This brown, dusty hardwood floor became my only true friend. I had a girlfriend at the time who was very kind and loving and I really cared for this young lady as well, but apparently (being as though she is not my wife today) all of those things weren't enough to sustain the girlfriend-boyfriend thing we had. On this salty dry cold hardwood floor I realized that it was not her, but it was me that caused the wedge between that relationship and many others. My life choices got me to where I was- alone, cold, womanless, hopeless, purpose-filled but unaware, and desperately homeless. This lonely, basement

apartment room in southeast Washington DC became my only source of strength, so I thought. While lying there, I heard a faint familiar voice speaking to me. It said, "Embrace it! Embrace it!". At first I ignored the voice until it continued to grow louder and louder. It forced me to acknowledge it and I spoke back: "Okay I embrace my mistakes; I embrace what I have done; I embrace the fact that I brought me here". All of a sudden, in a moments time, the floor became soft like a California pillow-top mattress and a strange thing happened to me. I fell asleep and I began to dream again. It normally would take me hours to fall asleep but on this particular day, it was as if I had taken some sleeping pills because I went out! The next day I felt rejuvenated enough to speak back to the faint familiar voice and I said, "I don't know what to do and how to move forward in life, I really want to progress and be a better person, have more and see more again, I want all of my hopes and dreams to come true, I want to have a beautiful wife with a life to match". The voice patiently responded in softer, yet clearer in tone, almost as if He was there with me lying on the floor. He responded by saying "Embrace it; embrace your life, Jahvon. Understand that your choices got you here and your choice will get you up from here".

This was a pivotal time for me in my walk with Christ for I had turned into a monster in many ways prior to this day. I was looking at life as if life owed me an explanation. It wasn't life's fault that I wanted to go off and be an idiot. It wasn't life's choice to do any of things that I had done prior to this day. What I discovered is that life is simply the benefactor of our personal choices. We either give life good things or bad things on which to live; the

choice is ours.

This all leads me to my point and intent of writing this book. I, once, was a young guy making the right choices, stepping into the correct places and then I stopped and veered off. Why? Because prior to that day, I, like many of the world's biggest idiots, had never seen myself the way God sees me. It wasn't until I didn't have anything but Him that I was able to see who I truly was. I realized that there is a potential inside of me that I had yet to tap into. My misery brought me to a place of seeing how much potential I had inside. My misery stripped me from all that I was a part of and helped me to uncover my purpose.

CHAPTER TWO

PURPOSE

Now, let's talk about uncovering your purpose more in depth. I have learned that every man has been implanted with a purpose. Every man also has gifts that will push this purpose to come to pass. These two things together are the fuel and oil that will keep your motor going once they are recognized and uncovered. The difficult part can be the uncovering piece. Day in and day out, I used to ask myself, what was I born for, what am I supposed do in life? I literally could feel the money and notoriety that comes along with operating in my purpose, but could not see how it would manifest. Heck, I couldn't even get myself to see myself having it all, but even in my lowest moments I could feel this purpose calling me. This purpose was bubbling on the inside, screaming, trying to get out! Webster's dictionary defines 'purpose' as "something set up as an object or end to be attained". The key on which I want you to focus your attention is the part, "something set up as an end". Very few people truly understand that there is a predestined place for us all to go in life. The amount of people that end up getting there is even greater. The unfortunate thing about both scenarios is that there are a greater number of people that never operate within their purpose; they often operate out of their talents. Talents are our gifts and the bible that I read says that your gifts can and will make room for you. With that being the case there are basketball players that should be lawyers and football players that should be pastors. Speaking of pastors, Dr. Creflo Dollar was a pretty awesome football player before he got injured. Who's to say he would have never found his God given purpose if he never got hurt? Maybe he acknowledged his calling way before college football. But what I do know is that my talents were

about to have me owning a nightclub or based on my experiences, a sin-club. I was all in and there was no stopping me, I just knew this was going to be one of the many things that my talents made room for. But my acknowledgement of the "end that was set up for me" placed me in a space that allowed for me to operate out of my purpose instead of my talents.

As we revisit the definition of "purpose", Webster's dictionary defines purpose as something "to be attained". If I am attaining something, that something can be possessed or achieved. The greatest accomplishment in life is to live a life that renders out the riches found in operating out of one's purpose. There is absolutely nothing more satisfying than to live life being paid to do what you are created to do. If King David would have shunned Samuel and stayed in the fields feeding the sheep, we would have never known Solomon. Yes David was very good with protecting the flock but he was an even better King. Why? Because he was able to fulfill his purpose while displaying his talents. We all have been created for something that is very necessary in the earth realm, the issue is the fact that many get caught up operating out of their talents instead of their purpose.

CHAPTER THREE

SPEAK

While climbing myself out of the hole of despair and anguish I had to lay a foundation for myself. I first had to speak positive reassuring messages to myself. In order for me to get up from this floor to take action and react to what I was receiving from God, I had to begin to tell myself that it was okay. I had to tell myself that all is well and that life was not that bad. My friend, Jamal Berry, would often ask me how I was doing. I would always say "awwwwww man, it's not that bad; it could be worst". He started asking about my well-being because he had seen that I was struggling; I was sad, sick and very weak in my approach to life. He knew that I used to be such a confident person. During the down turn in my life, I lost that swag I once had. It wasn't until I began to speak those things that be not as though they were, that things began to shift. I began to tell myself that this will

not be my bitter end, but rather my greater beginning. This was my race that I was running. I remember reassuring myself by saying "Jahvon, you've got to run the best way you know how regardless of the mistakes". I held on to that word every time I messed up. I kept telling myself that "this is not all, Jahvon; this is not who Jahvon Gordon is. You will be great; you are somebody. You are better than this; you are not a bum".

In this moment of my life I would consistently remind myself of how I ought to walk. If ever given to the opportunity to see me in person, I often walk with my head held high, and my chin up and chest poked out; it's all just a natural habit of mine. As a kid, I would always get teased for it, but in this dispensation of time, I finally embraced it. I began to really like the idea that I walked like this. I would remind myself of this walk and say, "Where you at Dr. Gordon? Show up!" Speaking these affirmations to me was the very thing that helped me think better about myself; I would speak differently about where I was going and ultimately I was able to see things differently. I was, for the first time in a very long time, very optimistic about where I was headed. I discovered that when you begin to speak differently about who you are and where you're going, you will see yourself rise earlier, stay up later and be energized longer. Nothing will be able to affect you in a long lasting way. People's opinion of you will become obsolete and you will begin to see yourself as being the Superman of your life, the superhero of your generation. You will begin to see that you have something to do on earth and you will be excited about doing it; whatever it is. People say all the time that knowing is half the battle. I add to that by saying, when you know you have a

purpose deep down on the inside, you will have the strength to uncover it. It all begins with speaking it first. There is a verse in the Bible that speaks heavily towards speaking those things that be not as though they were. This is very significant because it takes some very radical faith in that word to feel compelled enough to begin to speak over your own life. I can remember hearing a song that said "Speak over yourself, encourage yourself, in the Lord". I was so confused when I first heard it. I was like, "What?" and "How does that really work? How do I, a young man who is absolutely broke mentally, physically, financially, and emotionally, begin to speak about this crap? I don't even want to live it, let alone, speak about it!" Many people believe that it's talking well about oneself, as I did. What I discovered was that it was never about speaking well about yourself; it was all about speaking well about where you are headed. It's all about speaking about your future and what you envision. It was my misunderstanding and lack of proper insight to the fact that you can actually pre-determine your next steps all by speaking them into existence. Being a very sick child, I grew up thinking that I would have to be a very sick man. One of the Omega Psi Phi brothers from University of Maryland Easter Shore even named me, "Sick Wit It". It's crazy to think that I was so overwhelmed with illness until I discovered a word that said I can speak to my battle and tell it what to do. What?!?!? Yes I can speak to my body and it aligns with exactly what I say. I discovered that you can speak to your body, your finances, your family, your car, your "everything" and it will all begin to manifest into that which you have spoken. Try right now to begin to speak over something and believe in full faith that it will come to pass. You can even be bold enough to put a date

and time on it and watch how the authority that
God has rendered to you begins to reveal itself.

Keep It Elite

CHAPTER FOUR

CHARISMA

There is a purpose within you and the only way to uncover this purpose is to open your eyes up; I cannot stress this enough. Open up your inner eyes, your spiritual eyes, so that you are able to explore the "Charismatic You". There is a special charisma that we all possess, a special gift that we carry. This charisma is what people see while engaging you in conversation. This charisma is the very thing that keeps you going when all things seem to fall apart. The unique virtues that most people find to be weird are your charismatic characteristics showing themselves off. Long ago I accepted that I am a peculiar person and I, at times, do things that are a little out of the box. This peculiar nature has caused me to be a bit disconnected from the rest of the world, but once I found out that it was my charisma, I realized that I was never supposed to fit into certain circle. I began to operate in this new-found space. I discovered that most people knew it before I did and began to acknowledge me with words of affirmation. I would hear statements like, "I always knew that was in you" or "I knew that there was something different about you". All of which was good and bad but I didn't care because I understood, and still understand, that I am this way because of my peculiarity, gifts and the charisma that is found within me.

I am not saying that this separation from the world is the path for everyone. I just want to convey the point that everyone has a purpose and a gift within them. That gift is the driving force for that purpose. Think of your gift as the battery that starts the vehicle and your purpose is the vehicle that you must drive in order to get to your destination, or more specifically, your destiny. Using this gift to push that purpose that is attached to your vision is the only way to get to your destiny.

CHAPTER FIVE

ACTION

In life, you have to take action. You have to jump into action- just go wild with your believing and become bold enough to take on anything that comes your way. Be the action hero of your life! You want to be a real Transformer when it comes to taking back your world. You cannot sit back and allow life to take you over but rather you dictate life the way it's going to be. Life is about taking it not just simply making it, meaning, you can become a loser not because you aren't smart or because you are not cute, but because you fail to take the proper actions in order to win. According to Webster's dictionary, "action" is "the fact or process of doing something, typically to achieve an aim". I submit to you that the only way to uncover your purpose is to aim at something. Whatever your aim is, whatever your thoughts are about you and where it is you should be, make this your aim. Renowned motivational speaker, Les Brown, says "the problem that he had was not that he aimed too high and missed. The problem was that he aimed too low and hit". If you sit back in the pews allowing the rest of the world to preach to you or dictate to you what you should do and where you should go, you will only act on another person's dreams. This is what I have to say about that: Don't allow another man's thoughts of your future to overshadow your own aspirations in life. If you know that you are supposed to run for Senate, then go get'em, tiger! If you know that you are destined to play professional football, then go get'em, man! If you know that you are a writer, a producer, a rapper, an artist, a singer, a preacher, or even a teacher, then you tell yourself, "I'm going to get it!" But remember, you must take action. Robert Shculler once said "that no action is truly an action until a decision has been made. As a Les Brown Platinum Speaker, my road has not been easy nor has it been swift. I have seen long nights of wondering and hoping that someone or something would happen, but day in and day out nothing would shake. These things frustrated me, causing me to be very bitter and crabby about making it to where I was aiming. It was not until I began to become more optimistic about my abilities, my goals and my talents that things began to shake and move for me. It was when I took action and began to add my own friends on Facebook and create my own website that things began to change. I created my own motivational call instead of hoping to, one day get on someone else's call. It was not until I got into the face of adversity and confronted it, like the superhero that I am. It was then when I realized that in life, nothing was going to happen until I made it happen. No piece will move into this puzzle unless I place it there. People often say, "all the pieces will eventually come together". I beg to differ; nothing happens to those that sit and wait on others to place the puzzle together for them. People that sit and wait will end up being nothing more than an idiot sitting in the middle of the floor staring at pieces of cardboard. Life without action is futile and empty. Placing the blame on other people for your empty life is worthless and the people that place blame are merely followers, trying to drag someone else down to their miserable state of thinking and living. There is no room for the spoiled nor for the man who wants it in one shot. This race is for the men and women who want to succeed as much as they want to breathe. In order to be the action hero of your life, or of your situation, you will have to take extreme and radical action.

CHAPTER SIX

RADICAL

The best action heroes are those that are not afraid to take risks. Every great action hero has a "gangster" side to them. They are not afraid to take chances, risk the whole city to stop one villain, and talk some trash while they are doing it. They are risky because they are willing to temporarily wreck the life of the one he or she loves just so that they may save that loved one in the long run. However, I'm not suggesting that you scare your family off because you want to be stupid. The "gangster" attitude that I'm speaking of is like that of the mafia, that Godfather, "Scarface", "John Dillinger", type of gangster attitude. They all had this swagger about themselves that told the world that they could not lose. They always took the big risk by being bold. I need you to look at this from a very optimistic perspective and be open-minded with me here. I'm not gloating or boasting on the things that

they did or making any kind of, strong gestures where I am suggesting that you should become a killer or bank robber. However, what I am saying is this: in order for you to become the person you are aiming to be, you will have to be radical, meaning, not being afraid to take risks and walk with a "gangster" attitude while doing it. I'm suggesting that you need to be as cocky as possible, believing that you will make it, even if no one around you believes in you. You just tell yourself, "I believe in me". You have to be such a "smarty pants" about what you are doing that no one can tell you otherwise. You have to have cocky faith. Being radical does not come as a result of being loud, ignorant, and obnoxious. When you are living this Elite lifestyle, you allow your righteousness to speak for you. Your acts of righteousness will stop evil in its tracks and cause favor to reign supreme in your life. Often times our society has associated the word "radical" with "ridiculous". "Radical", According to Webster Merriam, means to be "very new and different from what is traditional or ordinary". Choosing to be Elite is not the norm nor is it the common way of doing things. This choice is one that causes immediate increase because of your aggressively radical approach to life. #WhatBox

CHAPTER SEVEN

COCKY FAITH

I once heard a teaching by Dr. Michael A. Freeman entitled, "Cocky Faith". In this series of lessons, he defined what the word "cocky" means in regard to the life of a believer. He taught within the series that the word "cocky" was synonymous to words like "swaggering", "smarty pants", "nervy", "know-it-all", and "arrogant". I reference this because I really loved how he shared the fact that it's okay to be these things as it pertains to leading a righteous lifestyle. He shares that every man has the ability to go above and beyond their everyday state of thinking and that everyone has a gangster inside that needs to be awakened. This gangster, of course, is this radical yet politically correct side of each of us that needs to come out. This person is the "Hulk" type of super hero. Understand that there is a Hulk inside of you that's ready to smash anything that is in your path to greatness. There is a gangster that

will take the risk and jump into action even when you don't want to. You cannot be afraid of this bold side of you. It is this side that will get you out of the boat and away from those that are too afraid to walk by faith and not by sight. This gangster is the deal-maker, the "go-getta", that you need in order for you to show up in the championship rounds of life and actually beat the breaks off the competition. There is no other way than the gangster, cocky way when uncovering your purpose and choosing to be Elite. Everything in life is a result of something else. The law of cause and effect states that absolutely everything happens for a reason. The process of receiving from your "Cocky Faith" works the same way. Let us look to understand what faith is. According to Hebrews 11:1, in the Holy Bible, we see that "Faith is the substance of things hoped for, the evidence of things not yet seen". As we analyze this cause and effect thing a bit further, we see that hope comes first and then faith. A persons hope is what is known to most as his/her vision or dreams. Let's take a moment to discuss the word "faith". Faith should be looked at as a verb or an action word. "Faith" in Hebrews 11 is given the adjective of the word "substance". Substance can be looked at as those actions that one must take in order to declare himself as acting on faith. When operating in this "Cocky Faith", you must walk around and confess that you're healed, rich, delivered, favored, changed, married or whatever you envision. Your faith is acting on what you believe God for. Your faith is exercised when you pay your tithes or give to the needy knowing that God will supply your needs. Faith is exercised when you go out and open a business account with zero clients. Faith is when you start a faith rumor that you are married and have a new house that you are closing on. Faith is

action not just words. Cocky faith is cleaning up your credit and, in the process, telling yourself, as you are reading the report, "Thank God for my 850 credit score". When you have a dream, and you want to exercise "Cocky Faith", then you have to go out and begin to act on what you see.

CHAPTER EIGHT

RELEASE THE "HULK"

Frankly, you need to know what you are and who you are. It's time that you "Get some weight in your step, man!!" For me, I walk into every situation knowing that I have so much to offer the other person. I operate in a spirit of boldness and certainty and I hold no punches. I make sure that in every conversation I am attentive and affirming, as well as, appreciative and assuring, while ultimately showing off what I have to offer. Often times I don't say a word. Why? There is power in the silence. I understand the truth behind the understanding of who you are on the inside and wearing it on the outside. Taking a look at women as an example. A woman can stop a room or shatter a glass just from her presence alone; however, men have the ability to do the same. My point is that all of these things start from who you are on the inside. Often times, I have to slow myself down when interacting with others because I tend to have so much I want to offer. My natural abilities allow me to find my way and adapt wherever I am. I am able to work with any and all people as long as they are open to share what they need. I am capable of doing these things because I work on being a strong-minded person, who is full of knowledge and capabilities. It is important to grasp the importance of walking around with a heart that is full and a mind that is empty and waiting for some deposits. Socrates once said that he walks around empty so that he may be made full. Let me help you to understand it a little further, a person who is willing to be taught operates in a spirit of humility. Socrates must have been a very humble person to desire to be filled up.

As the "Hulk", you want to know that you can explode out and pour out your vengeance of intelligence at any moment but it is so much cooler to walk around like Dr. Bruce Bannister and shine like the diamond, super hero you are. #KeepItElite

CHAPTER NINE

Board of Directors

Warning: This may just be one of the most important chapters of the book. Understand that you will acquire help along the way. There will be people that will come into your life for good and for bad. When you are operating in your purpose, there will be times when you don't know what to do with your vision. This does not mean that you were deceived in your thinking or that you have made the wrong move. It simply means that you must do one thing and one thing alone: you have to be open to receive the help of others. Now, understand that this help will come from all directions but with the help of the Divine Helper, the Spirit of the living God will expose you to the right people that will propel you to your next dimension. He will also dispose of those to whom you should never, ever be connected, but you have to be willing and bold enough to walk away from some toxic people and relationships. Be very serious about this because you can find yourself caught up in the wrong crowds that will slow you down. Hanging with people that have your problem will only bring you more problems. This may not sound like much but let me put it to you in question form: have you ever spent some time with someone and felt as if they are draining you? The conversation is one-sided and you end up becoming more like a teacher. This is a person that is not a real asset to your growth. They are the type of people that can help you, but not in the capacity that can add a skill or function that your skill set. This very well could kill your vision. There are such things as "vision busters" aka "vision killers". You will hear stuff like, "Aww man, you ain't got what it takes" or "That's impossible" or "No one has ever done that before – what makes you special?" You have to be able to speak to the voice of defeat and tell it to

SHUT UP! Gangstas have the attitude that says, "If I cannot get it myself, then I am resourceful enough to find out who can". In life, you always want to have a "board of directors" - people that are smarter than you, wiser than you, better than you in the areas that you are not well-versed. This is a very important step that you want to take. Why? Because you do not know everything nor will you ever know everything. There will always be someone that is smarter, taller, bigger, and stronger than you are and that's okay. What's not okay is for you not to accept this step of the process.

Keep It Elite

CHAPTER TEN

BOLD

You have to operate in an absolute spirit of certainty. You have to tell yourself that there is no way that I will not win when I operate in boldness. Being bold will get you into places that money cannot buy, where status can only take some and where very few will ever see. When a man is bold he can take over a nation and do it with ease. Look at Hitler, Michelle Obama, Lil Wayne, TD Jakes, Malcolm X, and Jesus The Christ. Of course all of these people are significantly different, but the point I am making is that they all are radical thinkers with a "gangster" attitude while they walked in that boldness. They all have an unstoppable, swaggering mindset that refuses to lose. They are all gangsters in their own way. Note that I am not subscribing to any of their movements in particular, I am just using them in a very practical way for observation purposes. So what's my point? All of them have an unfailing mentality that no man can contest. They, in their own right, are world changers. Very little is known to what was the key thing that struck the match and flicked the switch to "ON" for these guys, but what I do see is that they were willing to be bold enough to stand up for what they love the most. Whether these things were good or bad is a different story; my intent is to merely point this out to you. Nothing can supersede the amazing tenacity of bold people. (And that's Gangsta) Billy Graham once said, "When a brave man stands up, the backs of others are stiffened". (Now that is really Gangsta)

In order for you to make it to your glorious end, which is uncovering your purpose in life, you are going to have to be radically bold, being significantly gangsta in a very cocky, yet righteous kind of way. No man will stop you. No woman can road block your view. No word will hurt you. No situation will faze you because it's set in your heart to do it. You will know it like you know your last name. This desire to be great is so implanted into your make up that you will move any mountain to see it come to pass. When asked about it, you will be able to expound on it as if you were waiting for someone to ask you; you will know it by heart. Once you get to this place, you are absolutely ready to walk in your purpose and maximize your life. There will be nothing that anyone can do about it; they won't be able to stop you from the positive reassuring voice of your purpose whispering to you, saying, "Keep pushing and be bold about it". No one thing will be able to shake, rattle or roll you off your course when you are aware of where you must go and why you must be there.

#KeepItElite

CHAPTER ELEVEN

SLEEP CAN'T EVEN HOLD YOU

When your purpose is the driving force behind why you do what you do, you will begin to be mad at your sleep. The anger will come into play because you will consistently find yourself working throughout the day and night uncovering things and discovering new things that will be very interesting to you. Sleep will potentially be the only thing that will, at times, stop your flow when uncovering. Be very understanding to this fact; it will cause major disruptions to your process. Why? It is because you are going to find yourself wanting to release your potential without any kind of interruptions. Just know that this is constructive anger and you should express it. You should get upset with sleep because it will demonstrate to you the amount of dedication you have to a thing. Les Brown says it like this "IF YOU WANT A THING BAD ENOUGH, TO GO AND FIGHT FOR IT, TO WORK DAY AND NIGHT FOR IT TO GIVE UP YOUR TIME, YOUR PEACE AND SLEEP FOR IT".

I can recall late nights writing this book and falling asleep on my table and at the computer then waking up after dozing off and being very upset because I knew that I wanted so desperately to get this book out to the world. Sleep cannot be an option when you are working to be "Elite". You will have to burn the midnight oil and you should burn it so that you can properly obtain all that you should from this process. There may be days that arrive when getting sleepy and falling asleep become troublesome to your productivity. When you awake from a slumber at your computer screen or at your dining room table, after days of grinding this purpose out of your soul or when you have not eaten a great and hardy meal due to your focus, this is how you know that you are really working the uncovering process. Sleep is now known as your enemy because it is the one thing that you can find yourself trapped in. Sleep is the one time in life that you are allowed to lay down for your dreams and you should dream and dream Big. But if all you do is dream, your greatest lifestyle will only be a fairytale. DO NOT ALLOW SLEEP TO MAKE A BUM OUT OF YOU!

You will find yourself growing tired when uncovering things from within. The work you put in will be very tiresome and redundant at times but the fact that you must lean on is this: know that you have found the key to your destiny; know that this alone will keep you from sleeping. TD Jakes always says, "Success never feels like successful". I love his saying not just because it's true, but also because I believe every person can relate to it. Of course this does not happen to everyone but what I do know is that when you are after something amazingly great in your life, sleep is the one thing that seems to get in the way. You can lock yourself away from the entire world but you cannot get away from sleep. The point is that it's okay to sleep, but it is not okay to be okay with sleeping- sleeping on your work, sleeping on your drive, sleeping on your motivation, sleeping on your purpose!

CHAPTER TWELVE

THE OUTCOME

Believe that your purpose will keep you up and energized, fueled with excitement because, for once in your life, you know you're going in the right direction. Life will become simplified and even the geometry problems of life will flow like water. You will feel your heart burning on the inside as you meditate on this purpose night and day. The foreign linguistics that once probed your mind will be null and void and for once, every thought will be conducive to the direction in which you have them set. I'm not saying that you won't get bad thoughts thrown into your mind at times, but the point is that the options to do wrong will be minimized because you will be so focused on being "Elite". You will find yourself happy in the sad times and focus in the most unusual of situations. I can remember the day when I found this purpose and it really sank in for me. I listened to a review of about 3 songs on

repeat. I was so thrilled in knowing that the one thing I had always hoped, for had shown up. My faith was fulfilled and I was no longer a man that was empty. I was riding on the metro, smiling and cheesing, as if I had won a million bucks. The sky was brighter than ever and my inner man felt free. I wanted to go to work again because I knew that this was not my bitter end. I saw everything shift for me as this purpose revealed itself to me. This, too, will happen to you, if it has not already. Times of dismay will turn into learning moments on the inside while the rest of the world marvels at your transformation. People will look at you in a different light all because they see your inner glory beginning to shine. You will barely notice it because you are so engulfed with the knowledge of your future. Remember what TD Jakes said, "Success never feels like Successful"; therefore, stay

Keep It Elite

grounded and keep it elite!   #KeepItElite

CHAPTER THIRTEEN

WHAT DOES IT ALL LOOK LIKE?

James Scully said, "Dream big dreams and as you dream so shall you become". So as this dream world unveils itself into your fruitful life, you will begin to step into a whole new dimension called "My Purpose". Your Purpose will feel like you've been here before as you begin to float around in this new space. Things will come your way as you begin to exchange your purpose-filled smile with currency from those that are benefactors of your God-given gift. The word of God reads that the gifts of the Spirit are without repentance. (Romans 11:29). Understand that before you were even born this thing had been waiting on you to uncover it. Even my words of inspiration and teachings of empowerment were formulated before I was born. These words are not merely those intended to make you feel good about yourself but rather to give you hope. My intent is to fill you up with fresh living waters like the springs of Lebanon so that you may grow. This is not a game nor is it a fallacy unlike other self-help, motivational books. This is the inspired word of God. It is intended to stir you up to pull this "gangsta" out of you so that you walk around with the mind of God; the mind of Christ. (Philippians 2:5). Paul did. The disciples did. They were born of women and they lived on earth too, so why not you? Many say they don't believe in the Word of God and that Jesus is not the Son of God. Even if he were a mere man, no one can contest that he was not a very, brilliant man, with a plan to Keep It Elite. If Jesus created a life that was beyond human reasoning and he was able to think like the heavenly Father, why wouldn't I want the mind that existed in Him (Christ)?

OKAY MAYBE NOT YET & YOU'RE STILL LOST!

If given the chance to walk around with your same purpose that you possess, but with Einstein's brain, wouldn't you do it? Einstein invented the light bulb, but Jesus is the light in the bulb of this world. Einstein is cool but I'm rolling with the light that destroys darkness. That's my story and I'm sticking to it.

#KeepItElite

CHAPTER FOURTEEN

WHAT'S NEXT?

Let's continue with this major change that is happening to you. As you grow and show yourself approved, you will definitely "fail" your way to success. Furthermore, you will discover for yourself that success doesn't quiet feel like successful as I stated before. I believe in order to pull it all out; you will need a consistent, focused attitude that comes along with being seriously serious about living…about being Elite! Understand that these things take time and will only work for those that are willing to work the process. You have to work the process in order to gain the promise. Understand that the uncovering process is far more than just finding out what it is that you're supposed to do, right now, in life. This process is a life-long, slow roasting, fulfilling meal that will drop you on the plate of your destiny. Many men get to the surface of their purpose but never get around their actuality. The last couple of chapters will explore the stages of uncovering your purpose. The difference between people that are successful and those who fail in life is simply made up minds. When you make your mind up to become great, to be your best, to do your best, nothing and no one can stop you. The key to maintaining this lifestyle is having a made-up mind. I have stated this several times throughout the book. I once was told that if I continuously hear or see something, then I need to take note. You will now know exactly what it means to be tempted in areas that you had no idea that you could. You will see things pop up that never were issues before. There will be people that will begin to just hate you and others that will love you that once hated you. It all will be smoke and mirrors, or as Solomon would say, vanity. Understand that all of these things are distractions designed to get you off course. Jesus was tempted with every temptation imaginable and it all was get him off of His righteous choice to be Elite. Know and understand that none of these things can be avoided because distractions come to us all. Have faith in what you know to be true as you continue to maintain in your choice to be Elite; therefore, "Keep It Elite"

CHAPTER FIFTEEN

BELIEVE

You must believe that your life has been created for a very powerful reason. When Dr. Mike Freeman started The Spirit of Faith Christian Center, he had 12 members. When I began going to his church it had to be all of 150 people attending kids included. He began in Anacostia High School in Southeast Washington, DC. Every Sunday, this man showed up as if he was showing up to one of the three churches he now pastors and operates. You would have thought he was speaking to thousands in that hot auditorium. You could feel it in his words that he believed that one day he would have thousands of partners and a church large enough to host conferences and concerts. He believed that one day his voice would be broadcasted across the nations, speaking power and truth into the lives of people. I'm sure that he felt faint at times but that didn't matter to him; it was his belief in his "WHY"! It mattered not how he would get there, what mattered to him was WHY he was going to this undiscovered place. You have to believe in what you speak. Words are way more powerful than what we make them out to be. Our words are invisible but yet very powerful. Our words can tear a person down or build them up. Let's use God in this scenario to vividly show you how powerful our words actually are. When you think about the infinite power God has, you can imagine that his power is unstoppable. Looking into the book of Genesis 1, verse 3, "God said", then verse 6, "God said", then verse 9, the same thing. This pattern continues until verse 31 when God saw. So the remarkable, Most High God had to work the process of belief in what he said until he saw the manifestation of what he said. WOW! Words and the power of the belief you put behind those words can create a world that is irreplaceable.

I submit this to you, if you believe in the words YOU speak, you will become that very thing. Tell yourself positive reassuring things and really believe in what you say. Believe, now, on the positive and drop the negative in the trash. Step up to the challenge hidden in the belief system and uncover your purpose... Now!

CHAPTER SIXTEEN

RECEIVE

Once the manifestation arrives from your speaking and believing, it is important to maintain the proper posture to obtain the things that you spoke. Receiving begins with humility. Humility is one of those things that will get you into any door in life. Everyone enjoys the company of a person with a humble heart. Humbleness, while receiving your greatest lifestyle, will render you the unexpected things that life has to offer. Many humble people receive things just because others like the way they carry themselves. Humility will cause you to serve others in excellence as well. Serving is a perfect way to receiving the blessings that come along with your purpose. Understand this: every one of us needs people to push our visions. The best way to reap the harvest of servitude is to first be an effective servant yourself. Proverbs 29:23 says it like this: "A man's pride will bring him low, but the humble in spirit will retain honor" (KJV). Here, the word "low means to be humbled, to make low or sit down. As we know, pride will get you in trouble or as some have said, "Pride will get you nowhere". Now that you have decided to be Elite, know and understand that there are rules to this engagement. I will not go through all of them, but just know that the number one rule is this: the further you go up, the further your pride must come down. No one follows a leader who sees himself higher than he ought to. There is nothing wrong with seeing yourself high; just realize that increase and promotion come from the Greater one, not you. So what does all of this mean? The point that I am driving out is that you have to maintain the right posture in order to receive the things that God has promised to you in life. Our purpose has rewards when we operate out of them, one of the most important aspects is the happiness found in humility.

CHAPTER SEVENTEEN

REALITY

Life is merely a series of fortunate steps that we humans are privileged to live. Lucifer envied us and even the Angels questioned God about us. King David posed this question: "What is man that You are mindful of him"? I submit to you that King David, like many of us, was living in his reality and not his actuality. The actual fact is that we, as humans, cannot fly, spin webs, shoot fire from our mouths nor generate energy from our feet, but what we humans do have is dominion and power. These things were given to us before the foundations of the earth. God gave us the power to reign and rule over this world. The truth is that you can never lose in life when you understand that everything works to the benefit of your very being. There is nothing that can stop your flow or flowing into your next dimension. Never lose focus of the goals at hand. Realize that you are a self-made King or Queen– an ambassador of God. Understand that God breathed himself into you. His breath gave you life; His life now lives on the inside of your human package. Your make up is the only make up that could sustain in the earth realm. Of course, He could have made you just spirit like Him but instead He got Gangsta with it all and made you from the clay of the earth; he molded you a body to house your god-like spirit. This is not a hard concept to understand nor is it a difficult one to accept, but reality will keep you from getting it. One's perspective is their reality. If you keep looking at your skin, at your hair, at your circumstances, at your speech, instead of your spirit, you will always dwell in reality. Realities are things that you can see with your physical eyes. Well, guess what? Your eyes can and will deceive you. You have to open your eyes by taking off the blinders, and the restrictions that have held you back from seeing what is possible for you. Researching your spiritual identity within the word of God (The Holy Bible, Genesis 1-5) will reveal much of what I am sharing with you. You can live a free life through Christ by understanding your role in the program by, first, getting away from what you consider reality and, then, tap into actuality. Television and movies will tell you that you are a man with a soul and that's it. Life will try and make you feel as if you have no control over the issues that come up, but guess what beloved? You have reign over every terrain. I once saw a man steal the meat from a lions' mouth and all he did was walk tall and remain bold. It was all about being bold, self-confident, and taking dominion over the space that the lions occupied. Before you move further into this reading, use your computer or smart device to watch this clip on YouTube and you can get a glimpse of what real dominion looks like: http://youtu.be/Gz8msryNFCc.

I'll wait....

Welcome back! Now that you have seen what your life is supposed to look like, you can now go out and really take the world by force. I really like this video because it shows three men all working together as one. Like those three men, we, too, are three parts working as one: Soul, Body and Spirit. Our spirit man is the eldest of the pack and should lead to the way like the older gentlemen in the video, while the two follow suit. Man was nothing until he received the Spirit of God into his body. Understand that there is no way that the body or soul can lead effectively. The body is receptive to life's miseries, like sickness and disease. (Go back to Genesis for verification purposes) Let's make this video practical. The lions are life and the wildebeest is your finances. It seems that all is okay until WHAM… life hits your account. What do you do? Just sit back and allow your finances to get wiped out or do you stand up and put a demand on your finances by taking control of the situation? You're darn gone right! You must stand up for your finances and demand that they do what you ask for them to do. You can't allow the lions to eat up your wealth. The bible talks about how the enemy is like a lion on the prowl looking to devour all that he can. I urge you to do this: like that old man Rikita and his young tribesmen, walk up on that enemy, take what's yours and don't look back in fear. Stand up and see what is actually in front of you. Stand strong and always look to be great in every situation that you are in. Regardless of how the enemy is attacking you, look that mean ol' enemy in the eye and you tell him who the boss is. #KeepItElite

CHAPTER EIGHTEEN

ACTUALITY

This is the skinny of this whole matter: you have a purpose just like everyone else. There are no shortcomings when it comes to this, no one has been cheated or jipped. We all have a place to be and a part to play. The greatest thing that we can offer ourselves is to know the actual truth, which is this: there is no other way of seeing or believing other than what I have laid out to you in this book. As long as you live, you will always have this purpose living on the inside of you and there is no escaping it. You can't even live life fully without tapping into this purpose. You can make millions and billions of dollars and never tap into the real purpose of your life, finding yourself empty from the void of your purpose being unfulfilled. It will be pretty tough having fun and hearing your spirit man yearning for some assistance from the greater one. The beckoning of your spirit will help you to

get over to that next dimension- that next million or

your next wealthy place. I will leave you with this, it would really stink to live life and die and once you are at the judgment seat of Christ and he exposed to you that you could have made two billion dollars a year instead of two million dollars a year only if you would have tapped into what was actually available to you through your purpose.

CHAPTER NINETEEN

POTENTIALITY

Potentiality is dictated by the amount of faith you have. Every man has been rendered the same measure of faith according to the word of God through and by which the Apostle Paul explains in Romans 12:3. When you look at what levels and dimensions your life is capable of reaching, you have to know that those places are beyond measure by any man's thinking. This is all dictated on the amount of faith you are willing to exercise within yourself. Your potential can never be measured by any man nor by your past situations; it is measured by your right now mind. Whatever your right now mind tells you, wherever your right now mindset can perceive you, it will dictate the amount of potential you have. You can be a person who use to fail every course and drop the ball on every task that you were ever given and, one day, wake up with a renewed mind and get straight A's. This is all dictated not by what you thought of yourself yesterday, nor by what you currently see; it's all about what you believe you can become. What faith within a man can produce is far beyond the measure of human reasoning. It requires Kingdom thinking. In potentiality, you are going to have to put on your kingdom thinking cap. In elementary school, they used to say to us, "Put on your thinking cap" and we all would pretend to put on these make-believe hats. This is pretty silly until you find yourself as a grown up having to apply that very principle in your day-to-day life. In this new life that you are now participating, you are going to have to put on your Kingdom cap so that your thinking can come up. Your thinking will have to be in a different place. You will have to think the way God thinks so that you may receive the very blessings that God originally intended for you to receive. Do away with human reasoning and adapt

Kingdom thinking by having a heavenly mindset. Prior to everything you do, everything that you participate in, everything that you think, you must, first, ask yourself, "How would Jesus respond to this"? How would God answer that? Would either of them sit back and allow the devil to steal their stuff? Would either of them sit back and allow the enemy to speak to them, and would either of them not speak the back? You better cold believe that God and his arrogant ways would whip the enemies butt with His word; history proves that statement to be true. God always spoke back while in any situation, regardless of the circumstance. You, too, have to respond to life the same way, by first thinking with your kingdom mindset and then responding accordingly. If life tells you that you can only do this or you can't do that and you clearly see more for yourself, you speak back to life and speak out on that thing; addressing the matter with heavenly descriptive words of power that can only be inspired by those that are from up high. It is the only one way to live out your potential. It is also the way to remove the inner critic, the outer hater, and the negativity of the world and maintain a kingdom mindset that is unstoppable.

Be a gangsta, why don't you?   #Keepitelite!!!!

CHAPTER TWENTY

CONCLUSION

Don't allow life to win when you have so much potential to be so great. Actuality is waiting on you to come into it and see what really exists for you in the universe. It's time for you rise up and take dominion over this life of yours. It's time for you to receive "Your Great Awakening". It's time for you to believe in your purpose, and it is definitely time for you to achieve your greatest lifestyle ever. Always remember, while operating out of your purpose, to always have a reason to fight for your future by taking responsibility for your life while having the resolve to always Keep It Elite.

Keep It Elite

FROM THE AUTHOR

Thank you Mr. Les Brown for believing in me and showing me how to get my story out so that the world will be a better place. I will forever be hungry and ready to exude my greatness!

Contact Information
speak@jahvongordon.com
www.jahvongordon.com

Facebook
www.facebook.com/jahvon.gordon.5
Twitter
@Jahvondrgordon
@KeepItElite
Instagram
KeepItElite
LinkedIn
Jahvon Gordon